Assisted

Suicide

Essential Viewpoints

ASSISTED
SUICIDE
BY LILLIAN FORMAN

Content Consultant
John Henning Schumann, M.D.
Assistant Professor of Medicine, Section of General Internal
Medicine, MacLean Center for Clinical Medical Ethics,
Human Rights Program, University of Chicago

ABDO
Publishing Company

CREDITS

Published by ABDO Publishing Company, 8000 West 78th Street, Edina, Minnesota 55439. Copyright © 2008 by Abdo Consulting Group, Inc. International copyrights reserved in all countries. No part of this book may be reproduced in any form without written permission from the publisher. The Essential Library™ is a trademark and logo of ABDO Publishing Company.

Printed in the United States.

Editor: Andrew De Young
Copy Editor: Paula Lewis
Interior Design and Production: Nicole Brecke
Cover Design: Nicole Brecke

Library of Congress Cataloging-in-Publication Data
Forman, Lillian.
  Assisted suicide / Lillian Forman.
    p. cm. — (Essential viewpoints)
  Includes bibliographical references and index.
  ISBN 978-1-60453-056-8
  1. Euthanasia—Juvenile literature. 2. Euthanasia—Moral and ethical aspects—Juvenile literature. I. Title.

  R726.F64 2008
  179.7—dc22

                                        2007031916

TABLE OF CONTENTS

*In the 1970s, Joseph and Julia Quinlan
asked that their daughter be taken off life support.*

CHOOSING HOW AND
WHEN TO DIE

Assisted suicide is a fairly new concept in society and one that is surrounded with controversy. The most common form of assisted suicide is doctor-assisted suicide, in which people suffering from deadly or painful diseases ask their doctors to relieve their suffering by ending their lives. Although assisted suicide is legal in certain parts of the world, in most places the debate about whether it should be legal continues.

Assisted suicide is closely related to the concept of euthanasia. The word *euthanasia* comes from a Greek word that means "good death." Euthanasia can take many different forms. In what some people call "passive euthanasia," for example, a doctor will let his or her patient die, ending that person's life by letting nature run its course. Assisted suicide, in which a doctor or a family member takes active steps to end another person's life, is another form of euthanasia.

Some people euthanize their sick or severely injured pets. Most people feel that this is the kindest thing to do for an animal that would have spent the rest of its life paralyzed or in pain. Humans, however, have more options than animals. Medications exist that relieve even extreme pain, allowing people to continue to lead rich and useful lives. It is also possible for medical researchers to discover a treatment that could cure the person's disease or improve his or her condition.

Despite these considerations, some people feel that they have a right to choose what they consider a dignified death rather than enduring a long and painful one. Many U.S. citizens argue that the Constitution, which protects their liberty and privacy, gives them the right to choose passive euthanasia or assisted suicide. In some cases, the law agrees with them. But since the right to choose euthanasia is similar to suicide, the law allows euthanasia with many qualifications.

The Death with Dignity Act

Only Oregon residents can participate in the Death with Dignity Act. An applicant must establish residency by showing a valid Oregon driver's license, a lease or deed of ownership in Oregon, or a recent Oregon tax return. Participation does not require a minimum time for residency.

In addition to living in Oregon, an applicant must be: 18 years of age or older, capable of making and communicating health care decisions for himself or herself, and diagnosed with a terminal illness that will lead to death within six months.

ASSISTED SUICIDE AND THE LAW

Legislators disagree on whether to legalize doctor-assisted suicide. In 1997, Oregon passed the Death with Dignity Act, which made doctor-assisted suicide legal in that state. Federal authorities, however, challenged this state law. In 2001, former U.S. Attorney General John Ashcroft claimed that the Death with Dignity Act violated federal laws governing drug use. In 2005, the case was

An Oregon woman demonstrates in favor of the Death with Dignity Act.

argued before the U.S. Supreme Court. In 2006, the Court decided in favor of the Death with Dignity Act. Currently, Oregon is the only state that has legalized assisted suicide. Other states, such as California, New York, and Michigan, have tried unsuccessfully to establish similar laws. The only country that currently allows doctor-assisted suicide is the Netherlands.

NATURAL DEATH ACTS

Passive euthanasia, however, is legal in the United States. In 1976, California became the first state to allow terminally ill people to refuse medical treatments that prolong their lives without improving their well-being. Today, all U.S. citizens, under the Patient Self-Determination Act, have the right to refuse medical procedures that delay the inevitable outcome of their illnesses.

Different states have different versions of the Patient Self-Determination Act. Collectively, these are known as "Natural Death Acts." Under these Natural Death Acts, people can sign an "advance directive" document that gives instructions to health care providers about the care they want if they become terminally ill or

Karen Ann Quinlan

The tragic case of young Karen Ann Quinlan publicized the right-to-die issue. In 1975, she collapsed as a result of drinking alcoholic beverages after taking tranquilizers. Although she stopped breathing twice for 15 minutes or more, she did not die. Instead, she fell into a persistent vegetative state. This means that her brain was so severely damaged that she could not think, was unaware of her surroundings, and could not recognize the people around her. The doctors had no hope of curing Karen or of improving her condition.

Her father requested that she be taken off the respirator that helped her breathe. When the hospital staff refused to do so, he took the hospital to court. After several friends testified that Karen had stated that she would not want to live without consciousness, the New Jersey Supreme Court ruled that the doctors must honor Mr. Quinlan's request. The court claimed that a U.S. citizen's right to privacy encompassed the right to decline medical treatment under certain circumstances. This case prompted many people to make living wills.

severely brain damaged. For example, a person may state that they do not want to be resuscitated if their heart stops or put on life-sustaining machines if their brain can no longer function. These documents often vary from state to state.

There are two types of advance directives. One is called a "durable power of attorney for health care." In this type of directive, a person gives instructions for their end-of-life treatment and also names a patient advocate—someone they trust to carry out their last wishes. The second type of advance directive is the living will. Living wills do not specify patient advocates but do specify instructions regarding end-of-life treatment.

The Heart of the Controversy

Even legal forms of euthanasia have provoked moral arguments. People opposed to euthanasia make the following arguments:

❖ Individual freedom does not include the right to kill oneself or anyone else.

❖ A good society will care for vulnerable people, such as the disabled, those who are near death, and the elderly.

* The job of a doctor is to protect and prolong life, not to end it.

Those who favor euthanasia argue:

* Life no longer counts as human life when its quality and meaning are gone.

* Personal autonomy includes the right to choose one's own death.

* A humane society will allow its members to choose dignified and painless deaths.

Doctor-assisted Suicide

Marcia Angell, M.D., former editor-in-chief of the *New England Journal of Medicine*, makes the following case for doctor-assisted suicide: "Oregon's law is about individual freedom to determine the time and circumstances of one's own death when death is inevitable in the near future. What could be a more fundamental right than that? Why should government, or a doctor, have the right to make that very private decision for anyone?"[1]

The details of these basic opposing arguments can vary according to personal, religious, philosophical, and political positions.

ETHICAL AND RELIGIOUS VIEWPOINTS ON ASSISTED SUICIDE

Ethicists study whether certain ideas or behaviors are right or wrong. Generally, ethicists take two sides on the question of euthanasia—the traditional side and the libertarian side.

Traditionalists strongly disapprove of assisted suicide. They accept passive euthanasia under certain, very strict conditions. They believe that life is worth living even when it involves extreme suffering.

Libertarians approve of euthanasia as long as the doctor's intention is to relieve the patient from unavoidable pain. Libertarians make no distinction between doctor-assisted suicide and passive euthanasia. They feel that the quality of a life determines its value. If a person is permanently incapable of responding to his or her surroundings, they believe that individual is not alive in any meaningful sense of the word.

These differing ethical principles sometimes combine with religious beliefs. Religious opponents of euthanasia claim that life is a gift from God. People must continue their life journeys through happiness and sorrow, pleasure and pain. They must have faith that all their experiences, even pain and

Doctor-assisted Suicide in the Netherlands

The Netherlands legalized doctor-assisted suicide on April 11, 2001. Although 90 percent of the Dutch population voted for the measure, many were afraid that legalizing assisted suicide would undermine the idea that life is sacred. Others worried that foreigners would flock to the Netherlands looking for the easy death their own countries denied them. Officials sought to calm these fears by pointing out that assisted suicide, though not legal, had long been tolerated in the Netherlands without attracting death seekers.

illness, will help them to develop spiritually.

Religious proponents of euthanasia argue that when God takes a person's consciousness, He has taken the person's life. Without consciousness, no one can develop either intellectually or spiritually.

How the Issue of Assisted Suicide Affects U.S. Society

As with the issue of abortion, U.S. society is split between right-to-life groups and right-to-choose groups. These groups debate questions such as:

Is Assisted Suicide Discriminatory?

John Jefferson Davis, a leading Protestant thinker, feels that libertarian ideas about assisted suicide disregard democratic principles: "The choice ... between the 'sanctity of life' ethic based on the idea of the image of God, and the 'quality of life' ethic based on brain function, is a choice between an ethic that protects all human beings in principle, and an ethic with a sliding scale of human worth based on estimates of intelligence and mental function."[2]

❖ Will the desire for a painless death undermine spiritual aspirations and respect for human life?

❖ Will strict interpretations of religious doctrines lead to the loss of individual liberty and privacy?

People consider these questions when they decide what political leaders to vote for. Political leaders, in turn, legislate the laws of this country and, thereby, affect the most personal aspects of American lives.

Dutch lawmakers discuss assisted suicide in Parliament. In 2001, the Netherlands became the only country to legalize assisted suicide.

*In medieval Japan, the samurai often
killed themselves rather than get captured.*

EARLY CULTURES
AND EUTHANASIA

ultures in different eras have not always
placed the same value on life that many
people in the western world do today. Historians tell
us that people from past eras felt that the deaths of
some people benefited society.

In ancient Greece and Rome, it was an accepted practice for parents to leave their disabled infants to die on hillsides. Society taught that by killing these children, they were eliminating weaknesses in the family or community. In many cultures, such as those in the ancient Near East, pagan Europe, pre-Columbian America, and ancient China, priests sacrificed people to their gods. The ancient Egyptians buried their dead pharaohs' servants with them in their tombs so they could serve their masters in the underworld. Men and women in ancient Rome, feudal Japan, and other societies believed that, to some extent, they could redeem themselves from dishonor by committing suicide.

EARLY OPPONENTS OF SUICIDE AND EUTHANASIA

These examples from older cultures illustrate the beliefs of the majority of people in those cultures. However, every society has its dissenters. During the sixth

A Roman Chooses Death

Pliny the Younger described an incident in first-century Rome illustrating the typical Roman's attitude toward suicide: "Titius Aristo has been seriously ill for a long time. ... He fights against pain, resists thirst, and endures the unbelievable heat of his fever without moving or throwing off his coverings. A few days ago, he sent for me and some of his intimate friends, and told us to ask the doctors what the outcome of his illness would be, so that if it was to be fatal, he could deliberately put an end to his life."[1]

century BC, Pythagoras founded a philosophical group. He and his followers were very interested in mathematics. But they also had strong views on ethical and religious matters. They believed that abortion and suicide should be prohibited.

Many philosophers—such as Socrates, Plato, and Aristotle—adopted Pythagorean ideas, including the objection to suicide. Christian thinkers were influenced by these later philosophers. Early church leaders, such as Saint Augustine (AD 345–430), condemned suicide as a mortal sin. Most Europeans accepted this belief until the Renaissance of the fourteenth through seventeenth centuries.

RENAISSANCE AND THE AGE OF ENLIGHTENMENT

During the Renaissance, increasing numbers of people learned more about the customs and laws of the ancient Greek and Roman civilizations. They began to question many ideas of their own era, including the idea that it was

Why Suicides Were Buried at Crossroads

In medieval England, executed criminals were buried at crossroads. Since suicide was considered self-murder, the remains of people who committed suicide were treated like those of executed criminals. This custom comes from an ancient ceremony in which criminals were sacrificed to the gods. Since they built their altars at crossroads, they killed and buried the sacrificial victims there. Early Christian Britons adopted this ritual. The famous gallows at Tyburn in London was an execution ground situated on a crossroads.

Pythagoras

sinful to commit suicide in order to escape a painful death or shameful life. In 1516, Sir Thomas More, an Englishman, wrote a book about an imaginary land whose institutions and customs he believed to be superior to those in Europe. He called the land Utopia. In Utopia, euthanasia was an approved practice.

During the Age of Enlightenment in the eighteenth century, more philosophers began to express the idea that suicide was a permissible escape from suffering. One of these thinkers, David Hume (1711–1776), wrote an essay titled "Of Suicide." He believed that people had a duty to commit suicide when their lives had become unendurable.

Arguments against Suicide

- Pythagoras (sixth century BC): Since God placed the soul in the body, only God can remove it.
- Plato (ca. 427–348 BC): Humans are the property of the gods and so cannot destroy themselves.
- Aristotle (384–322 BC): Suicide is a crime against society.
- Saint Augustine (AD 354–430): Suicide is blasphemous because it rejects God and His gift of life.
- Saint Thomas Aquinas (AD 1225–1274): Self-preservation is a natural law and must be obeyed. It is also a crime against God and the community.[2]

THE NINETEENTH CENTURY

In the nineteenth century, the development of new pain relievers such as morphine, ether, and chloroform stimulated renewed interest in euthanasia. Some people began to speculate that these painkillers might be used to end the lives of fatally ill or suffering people. In 1870, British schoolteacher Samuel D. Williams argued that doctors should practice euthanasia by means of the new anesthetics.

Williams argued that it was the doctor's duty to:

Island of Utopia, from Thomas More's Utopia, *1518*

administer chloroform … to put the sufferer to a quick and painless death; all needful precautions being adopted to establish, beyond the possibility of a doubt … that the remedy was applied at the express wish of the patient. [3]

The debate spread from England to the United States. Doctors in both countries opposed euthanasia. Many medical writers expressed outrage. An article in the *Journal of the American Medical Association* accused Williams of suggesting that "the physician don the robes of an executioner."[4]

Attempts to Legalize Euthanasia

In 1906, "An Act Concerning Administration of Drugs etc. to Mortally Injured and Diseased Persons" was brought before the legislators of Ohio. They voted against the act 79 to 23. Nonetheless, this attempt at legalizing assisted suicide received much public attention in the United States and abroad. The *New York Times* published emotionally charged editorials and letters both for and against the act. The *British Medical Journal* strongly opposed it and remarked that it "would inevitably pave the way to the grossest abuse."[5] After this flurry of protest, the debate over legalizing assisted suicide died down.

It flared up again, however, during the 1930s. In his 1931 Presidential Address to the Society of Medical Officers of Health, Dr. Killick Millard proposed a bill for the legalization of assisted suicide in England. Also during the 1930s, a group of English physicians established the Voluntary Euthanasia Society with the goal of legalizing euthanasia. In 1936, members of the House of Lords considered a bill to bring this about. The bill was defeated 35 to 14.

THE TWENTIETH AND TWENTY-FIRST CENTURIES

U.S. proponents of assisted suicide founded the Euthanasia Society of America in 1938. But the horrors of World War II and the Holocaust overshadowed the issue. It was not until the 1960s that concern over assisted suicide revived

A Doctor Describes a Mercy Killing

The January 8, 1988, issue of The *Journal of the American Medical Association* carried an article by an anonymous doctor. In it, he described being on night duty while serving his residency at a private hospital. A nurse called him to help a 20-year-old woman named Debbie, who was dying of ovarian cancer. All attempts to cure her had been useless. She had been taken off chemotherapy and was receiving only supportive care.

On that night, Debbie was experiencing a bad reaction to her medication and was vomiting and struggling for breath. When she saw the doctor, she said, "Let's get this over with."[7]

"I could not give her health," the doctor wrote, "but I could give her rest."[8] He then injected her with 20 milligrams of morphine sulfate. "Within seconds," he continued, "her breathing slowed to a normal rate, her eyes closed, and her features softened as she seemed restful at last. ... With clocklike certainty, within four minutes the breathing rate slowed even more, then became irregular, then ceased."[9]

The doctor ended his article with the words, "It's over, Debbie."[10]

significantly. At that time, the Euthanasia Society of America (now known as the Society for the Right to Die) began to write and distribute living wills.

> "If suicide be supposed a crime, it is only cowardice can impel us to it. If it be no crime, both prudence and courage should engage us to rid ourselves at once of existence when it becomes a burden. It is the only way that we can then be useful to society, by setting an example which, if imitated, would preserve every one his chance for happiness in life, and would effectually free him from all danger or misery."[6]
> —David Hume, 1783

In 1973, the American Hospital Association created the Patient Bill of Rights, which gave patients the right to participate in decisions about their health care. Many people started to become interested in writing living wills.

The United States came even closer to accepting some forms of euthanasia when the California Natural Death Act was passed in 1976. This act legalized living wills and protected doctors who obeyed dying patients' requests not to be given life-sustaining treatment.

Oregon's Death with Dignity Act legalized assisted suicide in 1997. As of 2007, no other state had passed a similar law. Passive euthanasia, in which a physician allows a patient to die naturally, has gained much acceptance in the United States. But the controversy over assisted suicide continues.

Philosopher David Hume's essay "Of Suicide" introduced ideas that are still talked about in the debate over assisted suicide.

Pope Benedict XVI, the current leader of the Roman Catholic Church

Religious Arguments against Assisted Suicide

People often look to their religious beliefs when they are struggling with difficult issues. Although not all religious people oppose doctor-assisted suicide, traditionally most of the world's major religions have opposed it.

The Roman Catholic Church

Since 1980, Roman Catholic scholars concerned with the issue of euthanasia have studied the *Declaration on Euthanasia,* a document prepared by the Sacred Congregation for the Doctrine of the Faith. It condemns, absolutely, all forms of doctor-assisted suicide.

The document also discusses the physical suffering that usually accompanies death. It mentions cases in which Christians have moderated their use of pain medication in order to experience "a sharing in Christ's Passion."[1] In these experiences, some Catholics believe that they can become more like Jesus by experiencing some of the pain that he felt when he died on a cross.

However, it also states that others should not inflict pain on dying people. Doctors should give their patients medication that will lessen the pain, even when those medications hasten death. The drugs should not, however, dull their patients' consciousness and prevent

"Today it is very important to protect, at the moment of death, both the dignity of the human person and the Christian concept of life, against a technological attitude that threatens to become an abuse. Thus, some people speak of a 'right to die,' which is an expression that does not mean the right to procure death either by one's own hand or by means of someone else, as one pleases, but rather the right to die peacefully with human and Christian dignity."[2]
—"*Declaration on Euthanasia*"

them from meeting obligations to family, friends, and God.

The document does allow the patient to refuse:

> forms of treatment that would only secure a precarious and burdensome prolongation of life, so long as the normal care due to the sick person in similar cases is not interrupted.[3]

THE GREEK ORTHODOX CHURCH

Although the Greek Orthodox Church is also opposed to assisted suicide, it has not expressed its opposition in a formal document. When questioned about the church's position, Reverend Stanley S. Harakas gave much the same position against assisted suicide as that held by the Catholic Church. One difference is that, according to the Greek Orthodox Church, doctors may not consent to a terminally ill patient's request to be taken off life support systems and be allowed to die. They may, however, remove brain-dead patients from life support systems. This is not considered assisted suicide because the machines are "simply keeping the dead body 'functioning.'"[4]

Letting patients die is only permissible when it is God's will that humans should die, says Harakas.

Then their "bodily functions ... break down completely and irrevocably, and machines continue to keep a dead body functioning as if it were alive."[5]

Similar to Roman Catholics, Greek Orthodox Christians believe that pain can be an important Christian experience, helping the person to experience some of Christ's suffering. Nonetheless, again similar to Roman Catholicism, Greek Orthodoxy recommends that doctors give their patients painkillers even if the drugs shorten their lives.

PROTESTANT DENOMINATIONS

Each of the Protestant denominations has different factions with varying views about assisted suicide. Factions that interpret the Bible literally tend to condemn assisted suicide as murder. Many of these distinguish between actively killing the terminally ill and allowing them to die by discontinuing life-prolonging treatments.

The Protestant opponents of assisted suicide believe that life is

Is Heaven a Temptation to Suicide?

The Lutheran "Report on Euthanasia With Guiding Principles" answers the question, "Why should people want to live in an imperfect world when death brings eternal life in heaven?" It says:

"The assurance of life after death offers no excuse for ending life at will by euthanasia. Jesus' healing miracles foreshadow this major paradox of history ... that the mightiest advances in medical care have been made in those cultures which have come most heavily under the influence of the Christian religion with its emphasis on the blessed hope of everlasting life."[6]

sacred because it is a gift from God. The *Report on Euthanasia with Guiding Principles* was prepared by a Lutheran Commission on Theology and Church Relations. It states:

> *It is within God's purview [scope] alone to decide on the moment when the individual is to share that life which lies beyond death. ... Within the context of this certain hope, mercy killing runs squarely against the grain of the will of a gracious Creator.*[8]

Islam

Islamic scholar Dr. Hassin Hathout states, "No justification for taking life to escape suffering is acceptable in Islam."[9] He bases this statement on the Islamic Code of Medical Ethics, accepted by the First International Conference on Islamic Medicine in 1981. According to this code, mercy killing is an atheistic act because it

Suicide and the Afterlife

According to Islamic tradition, people who kill themselves to escape suffering are damned. Dr. Hassin Hathout retells a tale about the prophet Mohammed (AD 570–632), the religion's founder, and his army: "During one of the military campaigns, one of the Muslims was killed and the companions of the Prophet kept praising his gallantry and efficiency in fighting, but to their surprise the Prophet commented, 'His lot is Hell.' Upon inquiry, the companions found out that the man had been seriously injured, so he supported the handle of his sword on the ground and plunged his chest onto its tip, committing suicide."[7]

Muslim worshippers gather at a mosque to pray.

assumes there is no life after death. It also points out that dying people need not suffer since medications exist that can relieve their pain.

Hathout acknowledges that medication cannot always relieve the worst pain. Sufferers can, however, win spiritual rewards by enduring it with courage.

The prophet Mohammed, the founder of Islam, taught, "when the believer is afflicted with pain ... God forgives his sins and his wrongdoings are discarded as a tree sheds off its leaves."[10]

Islam does not condemn doctors who cause death by accidentally giving a lethal dose of a painkiller. It also excuses doctors who stop treatment when it becomes apparent their patient is brain-dead.

Goses and Terefah

Jewish rabbis have studied law and, to some extent, medicine. In their consideration of euthanasia, they have analyzed various degrees of illness and created special terms for them. The term *goses* is applied to someone in the final stages of life. Someone who has been diagnosed as having an incurable disease is described as *terefah*. That person may or may not be near the point of dying.

Judaism

A continuing debate about the morality and legality of assisted suicide takes place among Jewish scholars. More traditional rabbis consider life sacred and do not approve of assisted suicide. With a terminally sick person, however, they believe measures that prolong life artificially may be withdrawn.

Less traditional rabbis have different opinions about assisted suicide. Many feel that dying people today have different experiences than dying people in the past. Medical technology can keep fatally ill people alive for a very long time. Therefore, some liberal rabbis believe that assisted suicide should be examined further.

BUDDHISM

The basic principles of Buddhism oppose assisted suicide. One of the most important of these principles is karma. In Buddhism, death is the path to another life. The quality of each life is determined by the individual's behavior in a previous life. Karma is the influence of a person's behaviors from a past life on their present life.

The Unification Church on Assisted Suicide

Reverend Sun Myung Moon was born in North Korea in 1920. Moon claims to have had visions of Christ and other holy figures who told him that he would help establish the Kingdom of Heaven on Earth. On the strength of this prophecy, Moon founded the Unification Church in South Korea on May 1, 1954.

The Unification Church believes that assisted suicide is wrong. One of the sect's revered texts, *The Tradition: Book One*, states:

"Until we reach perfection, ... God owns our lives. ... Our spiritual body grows through a reciprocal relationship with our physical body. Therefore, it is the Unification view that under the order of the universe, we should not willfully cut the connection existing between the body and spirit."[11]

The Church accepts passive euthanasia in cases where a person is severely brain damaged. In the case of competent persons who are terminally ill, however, assisted suicide is forbidden. They are advised to spend their remaining time on Earth preparing for the spiritual world.

Geshe Tsultrim Gyeltsen is director of Thubten Dhargye Ling, the Center for the Study of Buddhism and Tibetan Culture in Los Angeles. Gyeltsen explains:

> We Buddhists do not accept this idea of killing oneself or others. For us, killing is always negative. ... Killing will not remove suffering, because suffering is the result of karma. If the karmic influence still exists when a person dies, he will experience the suffering in the next life if it has not been finished.[12]

Some Buddhists believe that people whose brain cells no longer function should be allowed to die. This exception does not, however, contradict the principle of karma. When people are brain-dead, their experiences cannot affect the quality of their next lives.

THE VALUE OF LIFE

Assisted suicide brings the value of life into question. Religious people believe that each individual's life is worth saving and that a society not founded on this idea would be immoral. All major religions believe that life is a divine gift.

The Reverend Sun Myung Moon opposes doctor-assisted suicide.

In the Bible, Israel's King Saul killed himself by falling on his own sword.

CAN A RELIGIOUS PERSON SUPPORT ASSISTED SUICIDE?

Almost all of the different world religions support some form of passive euthanasia. Some religious people are beginning to accept the idea that doctor–assisted suicide as well as passive euthanasia should be allowed. In doing so, they do not feel that they are betraying their faith in God or their beliefs.

It is possible that more religious leaders support assisted suicide than most people realize. Gerald A. Larue, president emeritus of the Hemlock Society, wrote *Playing God: Fifty Religions' Views on Your Right to Die*. To gather material for this book, he sent a series of questions about assisted suicide to various religious leaders. Larue stated that many of these leaders refused to have their views publicized for fear of alienating their colleagues and congregations. The leaders who did share their approval of assisted suicide explained that they continue to believe in the sanctity of life and the overarching authority of God's will. But they feel that these principles cannot be applied today exactly as they were in the past. Because new medical treatments prolong life without preserving its quality, these leaders have found it necessary to reconsider their positions on assisted suicide.

Why the Christian Church Condemns Suicide

In their book, *A Noble Death*, Arthur J. Droge and James D. Tabor point out that Saint Augustine was largely responsible for the Christian ban against suicide. Augustine was strongly opposed to a Christian sect called the Donatists. In the late fourth and early fifth centuries, Augustine carried on a campaign against the Donatists. According to Droge and Tabor, Augustine's condemnation of suicide was, to a large extent, an attack on the Donatist reverence for religious martyrdom.

Does the Judeo-Christian God Really Forbid Suicide?

Some religious scholars feel that, at its beginning, early followers of Judaism and Christianity supported suicide in certain circumstances. In *A Noble Death*, Arthur J. Droge and James D. Tabor claim that there is no ban in the Bible against what they call "voluntary death." They cite several examples from the Old Testament in which individuals voluntarily accept death. Saul, for example, fell on his sword in order to escape a humiliating death at the hands of his enemies.

Early Christian Martyrs

In the early days of Christianity, the Roman empire persecuted Christians. In AD 203, one Roman governor threatened to kill a group of Christians if they would not practice the Roman religion. He took special pains to talk Perpetua, a 22-year-old mother, out of condemning herself to death. "Have pity on your father's grey head. ... Have pity on your infant son. Offer the sacrifice for the welfare of the emperors."[1]

But she refused, admitting freely that she was a Christian. After all the others had testified in the same way, the governor sentenced them to be killed by beasts and gladiators as a public entertainment. An anonymous narrator describes the day of their death as follows:

[T]hey marched from the prison to the amphitheater [arena] joyfully as though they were going to heaven, with calm faces, trembling, if at all, with joy rather than fear. When the beasts failed to kill the Christians, the crowd demanded that they be brought forward so they could watch the gladiators dispatch them. [Most] took the sword in silence and without moving.[2]

Could Assisted Suicide Elevate the Concept of Life?

To some extent, religious martyrdom might serve as an example of assisted suicide chosen for unselfish reasons. Christian martyrs wanted to show others that they were not afraid to die for their beliefs. Similarly, some terminally ill people believe that their deaths can help others. Often such people donate their organs to people who might live active lives if they receive transplants. Others simply want to save their family's financial resources.

A Jewish Leader's Reaction to Proposition 119

Some religious leaders disagree with assisted suicide but do not want to impose their beliefs on other people. In 1991, Proposition 119 proposed the legalization of doctor-assisted suicide in the state of Washington. Despite his personal disapproval of doctor-assisted suicide, Rabbi Anson Laytner, director of the Seattle Jewish Federation Community

A Jewish Martyr

The Jewish tradition also has its martyrs. The book of Maccabees describes a man who would rather die than eat pork, a meat forbidden by Jewish law: "Eleazar, one of the scribes in high position, a man now advanced in age and of noble presence, was being forced to open his mouth to eat swine's flesh. But he, welcoming death with honor rather than life with pollution, went up to the rack [an instrument that pulls people limb from limb] of his own accord, spitting out the flesh, as men ought to go who have the courage to refuse things that it is not right to taste, even for the natural love of life." (2 Maccabees 6:18–20)[3]

A Methodist Minister's Approval

The Reverend Arthur C. Campbell, a retired minister in the United Methodist Church, does not feel that his religion should condemn doctor-assisted suicide. He states that "he would take the choice of ending his life with a physician-assisted process if he were to be faced with a terminal and painful disease." His view is based on something his father said: "Our faith always holds in balance the respect for life, a reverence for it, with the quality of life. One without the other is contradictory."[4]

Relations Council, voted for its legalization. In general, Laytner believes that each individual Jew is free to write a directive asking to be taken off life-support systems if he or she enters a persistent vegetative state. Laytner would not, however, counsel anyone to request doctor-assisted suicide. He objects to Proposition 119 in particular because it permits someone to commit suicide at any time within the six months he or she has left to live. This goes against his conviction that one should "hold onto life as long as possible."[5]

Nevertheless, he supported the bill. As he explains,

> *Initiative 119 is not a Jewish initiative; there are people of other faiths whose religious views run the gamut from official opposition to 119 to official support for it. Although our tradition opposes aid in dying, far be it from us to impose our religious views on people of other faiths.*[6]

Unitarian Universalists Consider Assisted Suicide

Unitarian Universalist leaders have a policy to tolerate dissent about major issues among both their clergy and members of the congregation. On June 17, 1988, the General Assembly of the Unitarian Universalist Association adopted a "Right to Die with Dignity—1988" resolution. This resolution affirmed generally accepted right-to-die measures such as living wills and durable powers of attorney. It also supported aid-in-dying measures.

One Unitarian Universalist pastor, the Reverend Edgar Peara of Park Forest, Illinois, presented the case for the resolution by pointing out an inconsistency in the religious precept that life is sacred. If this precept is so binding, he argued, then warfare, killing in self-defense, and capital punishment should be forbidden as well. He also challenged the idea that assisted suicide frustrates God's will. If that were so, he countered, then curing what were

Changing Attitudes

Gerald A. Larue claims that religious leaders are beginning to lose the belief that "physician-assisted euthanasia is tantamount to 'playing God.' ... Chaplains ... are asking whether or not the churches or synagogues, in their response to modern medicines' ability to continue to keep terminally ill persons alive, might be the ones who are truly playing God. The refusal of support by religious groups of so-called 'heroic' medicine, and the endorsement of what is often called 'voluntary passive euthanasia,' constitutes a first step in abandoning the playing God role."[7]

once fatal diseases also frustrates God's will. Surely, if curing someone is an act of Christian kindness, then so is giving an incurable person a painless and speedy death.

HINDUISM AND ASSISTED SUICIDE

According to Swami Swahananda of the Vedanta Society of Southern California, Hindu leaders leave the choice of euthanasia up to the individual. They do not encourage euthanasia, but they do not forbid it either. They only advise Hindus to follow the laws of their country. Swahananda states that:

> In ancient India, that is in very old days, there were occasionally cases of sadhus [holy men] giving up their life in rivers or mountains. Of course, on very rare occasions.[8]

EVOLVING ATTITUDES

The Judeo-Christian attitude toward euthanasia has changed from acceptance in the distant past to firm disapproval in more recent times. However, nearly all denominations now accept passive euthanasia. More recently, some churches and synagogues have begun to have second thoughts about assisted suicide. ⁓

Indian Hindus pray in the Ganges River.

*Protesters gather in the Netherlands,
the only country to legalize assisted suicide.*

ETHICAL ARGUMENTS
AGAINST ASSISTED SUICIDE

any people believe that religious
doctrines cannot determine whether
a law should be imposed on a society of people
from a variety of faiths. Instead, they turn to ethical
arguments about legalizing assisted suicide. Like

religious leaders, however, ethicists are divided on the issue.

Traditional ethicists base their opposition on a premise similar to the religious idea that life is sacred— the difference is that ethicists do not necessarily consider life a gift from God. Because they believe that life is intrinsically precious, they conclude that it is wrong to actively take the life of an innocent person even in order to rescue that person from suffering.

Traditionalists view passive euthanasia as totally different from assisted suicide and do not include it in the same moral category. They argue that if doctors withhold treatment from terminally ill patients, the diseases, not the doctors, have killed them. Therefore, they believe that passive euthanasia is permissible when patients, on the point of death, ask that treatment be withheld. Doctors who engage in assisted suicide (by injecting

"[Assisted suicide] destroys the real, if abstract, values that connect us and make us human beings. Doctors would become executioners who make decisions about who [has] 'quality of life' and who [has] not. Disintegration would be being made whole again. Cowardice would become lionized as courage. The duty to make the most of what one has would become the duty to throw it away. The meaning of human life would be reduced to the physical, base animal instincts, trapped within the contours of the body. Human dignity would be reduced to bodily aestheticism."[1]
—*Kevin Yuill*

patients with lethal drugs, for example) actually cause their deaths. Traditionalists consider this form of euthanasia wrong even if doctors only help patients inject themselves.

Besides believing that assisted suicide turns the doctor into a killer and the patient into a suicide, traditionalists have another objection to the procedure. If the patient was not as sick as the doctor thought, the effects of assisted suicide cannot be reversed. Passive euthanasia, however, is reversible. If a doctor stops a life-preserving treatment and the patient does not die as expected, the doctor could begin the treatment again.

How Traditionalists View Human Life

When traditionalists claim that human life is intrinsically precious, they include all aspects of that life. They believe that even as people are dying, their lives continue to be important. Dying people still have a relationship with their families and friends and, for their sakes, should stay alive as long as possible. Dying people also have the responsibility to use their suffering as a means of developing and completing their own personalities.

A Doctor's Role

Traditionalists believe that doctor-assisted suicide carries with it psychological, social, and moral issues. An important cause of these problems is that, even when the doctor only provides the means of death at the patient's request, the doctor has taken a life. Many doctors object to assuming such a role. They became doctors because they wanted to heal others. All of their training has been focused on this goal.

In 1998, two physicians, Lawrence Hartmann and Arthur Myerson, debated whether doctor-assisted suicide should be made legal. In arguing against assisted suicide, Myerson told how as a boy he had admired Dr. Rosenfeld, his family doctor. He recalled that his mother had suffered from depression and a debilitating, but not disabling, bone disease. She asked Dr. Rosenfeld several times to help her

Euphemisms for Assisted Suicide

Rita L. Marker and Wesley J. Smith claim that right-to-die activists are replacing old terms with new ones to make the idea of doctor-assisted suicide more acceptable. They feel that this shows that people basically consider this procedure wrong. In their article, "When Killing Yourself Isn't Suicide," they write, ".... [Right-to-die activists] found that people have a negative impression of the term 'assisted suicide,' but, if euphemistic slogans like 'death with dignity' or 'end of life choices' were used to describe the same action, response was relatively positive. ..."[2]

commit suicide. Dr. Rosenfeld refused. Instead, he prescribed pain management and recommended psychiatric treatment. Myerson states that when Dr. Rosenfeld encouraged his mother to live, he gave her hope and the sense that she was important to her family. He had improved the quality of her life. Dr. Myerson feels that Rosenfeld embodied "the essence of physicianhood," a characteristic he feels that all doctors should strive to possess.[3]

Doctor-assisted Suicide and Medical Values

Ethicists fear that engaging in assisted suicide will cause doctors to be less concerned with protecting human life. Some experts fear that in Oregon, where doctor-assisted suicide is legal, many medical practitioners have lost both their sensitivity and their respect for rules. In 2005, the Physicians for Compassionate Care Educational Foundation published a paper that questioned the way in which doctors in Oregon were carrying out assisted suicide. They also felt that medical authorities were not adequately supervising the doctors. The members of this organization based their criticisms on an annual report on the procedure that the Oregon Department of Human Services published in 2004.

The report included the following criticisms:

❖ Only 5 percent of the people who had been helped to die had had psychiatric evaluations.

❖ Doctors sometimes did not tell the patients about alternatives to doctor-assisted suicides.

VULNERABLE GROUPS AND ASSISTED SUICIDE

Traditionalists point out that society often causes members of certain groups to feel valueless. These groups include the elderly, the disabled, the incurably ill, and the mentally ill. The members of these groups tend to be poor—often as a result of their

Stephen Hawking: A Life Not Worth Living?

When he was 21 years old, Stephen Hawking was diagnosed with Lou Gehrig's disease. This disease causes the death of motor neurons (the nerves that make the muscles work). As the disease progresses, the victim becomes paralyzed. It does not affect the heart, the digestive system, or the brain. Despite this severe disability, Hawking continued to live as fully as possible. Besides establishing a career as a brilliant scientist, he married and had three children.

As the years passed, Hawking became increasingly helpless and lost the ability to speak. He now uses an electric wheelchair. A friend sent him a special computer program that he can operate by head or eye movements. The computer also includes a speech synthesizer to enable him to talk. With his special computer, he has written groundbreaking books on astrophysics. Two of these were written for the general public. They are titled *A Brief History of Time* and *Black Holes and Baby Universes and Other Essays*.

Stephen Hawking, a renowned astrophysicist, has made many accomplishments despite a debilitating disease.

condition. Many require intensive and/or long-term care and cannot afford the kind of insurance that would provide it. Their families often consider them financial drains and cannot always hide this attitude.

Opponents of assisted suicide point out that society sometimes encourages people with disabilities to die. In her essay, "Not Dead Yet," Diane Coleman writes about the 1983 case of Elizabeth Bouvia. This young woman had cerebral palsy, a condition caused by brain injuries that occur before birth. People suffering from cerebral palsy typically have jerking movements in one or more of their limbs, paralysis of part or all of the body, and hearing, vision, and speech problems. At first, Bouvia coped well with her disability. Later, however, she experienced a series of crushing problems. She admitted herself into a psychiatric ward, where she declared her intention of starving herself to death and requested that she be given morphine.

Several psychologists supported Bouvia's right to die. They testified that Bouvia's desire to die was rational, that it was based on her disability rather than on a temporary state of despair. An activist group of disabled people protested against this evaluation. They claimed that the psychologists were treating Bouvia differently than they would treat a non-disabled person in similar circumstances. If she were not

"Euthanasia is a concept, it seems to me, that is in direct conflict with a religious and ethical tradition in which the human race is presented with 'a blessing and a curse, life and death,' and we are instructed ... 'therefore, to choose life.' I believe 'euthanasia' lies outside the commonly held life-centered values of the West and cannot be allowed without incurring great social and personal tragedy. This is not merely an intellectual conundrum. This issue involves actual human beings at risk ..."[4]
—C. Everett Koop, former U.S. Surgeon General

disabled, they said, the psychologists would treat her for depression and prevent her from committing suicide.

Doctor-assisted Suicide and Human Society

In his essay, "I Will Give No Deadly Drug," Leon R. Kass, M.D., Ph.D., points out that the legalization of doctor-assisted suicide will make hospitals even more frightening to people who are already rendered helpless by their illness. Kass also feels that legalized euthanasia would be harmful even to the people who want to die. He claims that it dehumanizes them and that only animals should have an easy death. Since humans have a complex consciousness, says Kass, death can be a profound and ennobling experience for them.

Preserving "Moral Health"

Most traditional ethicists agree with Kass that doctor-assisted suicide is a denial of the important human qualities of courage and responsibility. It takes away a person's last chance to act responsibly by setting his or her affairs in order and by expressing love for family and friends. By opposing the legalization of doctor-assisted suicide, Kass feels that "medicine may serve not only the good of its patients, but also, by example, the moral health of modern times."[5]

*Former U.S. Surgeon General Dr. C. Everett Koop
has expressed opposition to assisted suicide.*

Protestors demonstrate outside the U.S. Supreme Court in favor of assisted suicide.

ETHICAL ARGUMENTS FOR ASSISTED SUICIDE

*L*ibertarian ethicists do not believe that all levels of human life are intrinsically precious. Libertarians distinguish between biological life and biographical life. Biographical life is the sum of a person's desires, goals, interests, and relationships. Libertarians believe that doctors should be able to perform assisted suicide on people who have only biological life. In such cases, they believe that the doctors are not really killing the patients. The disease or injury has already done that by destroying their consciousness. All the doctor is doing is ending basic bodily functions that no longer have a human purpose.

Libertarian ethicists also believe that there is no difference between assisted suicide and passive euthanasia. Libertarians reason that actively causing the death of a dying person by a lethal injection or passively causing the death by withholding treatment is the same—the intent is the same whether it is assisted suicide or passive euthanasia.

HELPING PEOPLE END THEIR BIOGRAPHICAL LIVES

Libertarians point out that traditionalists consider it permissible to grant competent, willing persons the right to die by removing them from life-support machines. Why

Compassionate Care

In his essay, "Palliative Care and Euthanasia in the Netherlands: Observations of a Dutch Physician," Zbigniew Zylicz, M.D., tells about a woman dying of breast cancer. When she requested a lethal injection, the doctor asked her why she wanted it. She explained that she had an irrational fear of being buried alive. By allaying this fear, he helped her to choose a natural death. He thus showed that compassionate terminal care can be given in a country where doctor-assisted suicide is legal.

then would it not be permissible to grant them
this right by giving them a lethal injection? Passive
euthanasia seldom works quickly, and the patient
continues to suffer. Prolonged and needless
suffering defeat the doctor's intention to be
compassionate.

Libertarians also point out that people still in
possession of biographical life have autonomy. This
means that they can choose to do whatever they want with their lives as long as they do no harm to others. According to libertarians, it is morally right for such people to kill themselves or to obtain the help of others to do so. Therefore, they believe it should be legal as well. Libertarians feel

---

James Rachels, Ph.D., 1941–2003

A colleague described philosopher James
Rachels as a rare combination—"a good philosopher and a person who can think practi-
cally."[1] Many ethicists who support assisted
suicide and passive euthanasia have based
their arguments on Rachels' article "Active
and Passive Euthanasia" and his 1986 book,
The End of Life: Euthanasia and Morality.

In *Created From Animals: The Moral Implica-
tions of Darwinism*, Rachels discusses the im-
plications of Darwin's discovery that humans
share their origins with other animals.

*Human life will no longer be regarded
with ... superstitious awe ... and the lives
of nonhumans will no longer be a matter
of indifference. This means that human
life will, in a sense, be devalued, while
the value granted to nonhuman life will
be increased. A revised view of such matters as suicide and euthanasia, as well as
a revised view of how we should treat
animals, will result.[2]*

that the individual, not the state, has the right to decide whether their life is worth living.

Legalization Will Lead to Regulation

Another argument for legalization of assisted suicide is based on the knowledge that it already occurs illegally. Supporters of assisted suicide cite the many doctors who have anonymously confessed to giving pain-wracked, terminally ill patients enough morphine to kill them. Traditionalists express concern that assisted suicide, if legal, would be abused. Libertarians argue that legalization, far from causing abuse, would lead to proper regulation and supervision of the procedure, because doctors and patients would no longer have to practice assisted suicide in secret.

The Need to Examine the U.S. Health Care System

Those in favor of legalizing assisted suicide point out that abuses occur in alternatives to euthanasia, such as hospice care. In *Last Rights: Death Control and the Elderly in America*, Barbara Logue points out that bureaucratic and staffing problems often cause hospice patients to be neglected. In the following

example, she points out that, ironically, these
problems sometimes lead to covert assisted suicide:

> *A good illustration is the action of Montana's "Hospice
> Six"—six nurses accused of illegally dispensing narcotics to
> suffering patients, such as the one heard screaming in pain as
> the nurse drove up to his home and another found in a fetal
> position, soiled with feces, after waiting five hours for help.*[3]

Proponents of doctor-assisted suicide point out
that, even at its best, conventional medical care often
does not serve patients' best interests because the
U.S. medical model is too focused on prolonging
life. Advances in medical technology allow doctors
to go to unreasonable lengths in extending life. In
her book, *Last Rights: The Struggle Over the Right to Die*, Sue
Woodman asserts that it is difficult for nurses and
physicians to accept death. Woodman describes the
plight of an elderly woman who had suffered for
many years from heart disease and diabetes. At the
age of 90, she was becoming blind and deaf. She
also had gangrene in both legs and needed a double
amputation.

When faced with the prospect of losing her legs,
she said she preferred to die. The doctors agreed not
to treat her condition. They put her in a pleasant

room in which they expected that, surrounded by her family, she would die in two to three weeks. Nine weeks later, she was still alive—but just barely. She slept most of the time. When she was awake, she babbled confusedly. She was emaciated.

Nonetheless, the nurses and doctors did all they could to keep her alive. In addition to morphine for pain, they administered antibiotics and insulin. They fed her with nourishing fluids. But even though she was still alive, in her diminished state, she was incapable of setting her spiritual and material affairs in order. She could not express her love for her family.

Doctors in Denial

The belief in healing patients is so central to the health care industry that many health professionals see death as failure. Perhaps that is why many have a difficult time confronting death with their patients. A study published early in 1996 discovered that, despite 20 years of living wills and "do not resuscitate" orders, most physicians are still ignoring them and forcibly giving their patients lifesaving measures they do not want.

CAN CHOOSING DEATH BE A RESPONSIBILITY?

In his book, *Is There a Duty to Die? and Other Essays in Medical Ethics*, John Hardwig claims that dying people have responsibilities to their loved ones. He asks how much a dying patient's family should be expected to give up in order to delay another's death.

Hardwig illustrates this question by describing a common situation. An 83-year-old woman with terminal congestive heart failure insists on the most aggressive life-prolonging treatment possible. This treatment keeps her alive two years longer than the doctors had expected. In order to provide her mother with this treatment, her 55-year-old daughter sacrifices her life savings, her home, and her profession. Hardwig wonders if the mother had a duty to die rather than to ruin her daughter's life.

However, Hardwig acknowledges that the government cannot require individuals to fulfill their "duty to die." Making the choice to die or to prolong life involves many personal considerations and, therefore, must be a personal decision. According to Hardwig, individuals must learn to acknowledge their duty and to prepare their minds and hearts to take it on. He suggests that in order to determine if they have a responsibility to die, people should question if prolonging their lives will impose extreme hardship on their loved ones.

A Family Example

John Hardwig, author of *Is There a Duty to Die?*, tells about his grandfather's decision to commit suicide: "My own grandfather committed suicide after his heart attack as a final gift to his wife—he had plenty of life insurance but not nearly enough health insurance, and he feared that she would be left homeless and destitute if he lingered on in an incapacitated state."[4]

Hardwig does not believe that a mentally incompetent person, such as an Alzheimer's patient or a patient in a vegetative state, has a duty to die. How can an individual choose to die, he wonders, if he or she cannot even understand his or her duty? For this reason, Hardwig believes that individuals who know they will soon become mentally incompetent should end their lives while they are still able to reason.

The Rewards of Choosing Death

To Hardwig, being fully conscious of one's duty to die can give death dignity and meaning. In his words:

> *Recognizing a duty to die affirms my ... moral agency. ... Second, recovering meaning in death requires an affirmation of connections. If I end my life to spare the futures of my loved ones, I testify in my death that I am connected to them. It is because I love and care for precisely these people (and I know they care for me) that I wish not to be such a burden to them.*[5]

To some extent, Hardwig's ideas counter Leon Kass's argument that assisted suicide denies one's human dignity. Hardwig claims that if chosen for the right reason, dying deliberately affirms one's best human qualities.

Many people are shocked and intimidated at Hardwig's ideas. Certainly it would take a very strong-minded and determined person to carry them out. Nonetheless, even people who disagree with the "duty to die" believe that the idea has value. If nothing else, the idea points out the failings in the U.S. medical system. Hardwig points out that society is unwilling to "pay for facilities that provided excellent long-term care (not just health care!) for all chronically ill, debilitated, mentally ill or demented people in this country." If society was willing, "the duty to die would then be virtually eliminated."[6]

The issue of assisted suicide has brought many underlying problems into focus. It shows that these questions have no easy answers. ⌐

Effects of Prolonged Deaths on Patients' Families

In *Last Rights: Death Control and the Elderly in America*, Barbara J. Logue discusses some of the problems that relatives experience in caring for a dependent elderly person. She points out that such caregiving reduces the family's income, interrupts routine activities, and takes attention away from other family members. All these deprivations can affect the children of the household. It may set a good example for them of compassion and responsibility, but it might also deprive them of essential nurturing.

*Lynn Norton holds a picture of her friend John T. Welles,
who asked his loved ones to help him die.*

Dr. Jack Kevorkian

DR. KEVORKIAN

r. Jack Kevorkian, sometimes called "Dr. Death," defied the law by performing assisted suicide on people who were disabled and chronically or terminally ill. It appears that in most cases, he did so with his subjects' consent. In the course of his career, Kevorkian helped more than 130 people end their lives.

Some people think Jack Kevorkian is evil, while others believe him to be heroic and humane. Ethicists consider the issue of intent to be important when judging the morality of an action. They would ask if Kevorkian helped people kill themselves in order to gratify his own dark needs or in order to rescue them from mental and physical suffering.

The Death Rounds

Mass murderer. Angel of Death. Dr. Death. These names express the distaste that many people have for Kevorkian's actions. Even before he began practicing assisted suicide, his colleagues felt uneasy about his preoccupation with death. In 1956, at the age of 28, he published an article that discussed the state of a dying person's eyes. Kevorkian thought that the ability to recognize the effect that dying has on human eyes would enable doctors to determine when resuscitation was useless.

Kevorkian's Art

Kevorkian painted as a hobby. One of his paintings, *Nearer My God to Thee*, shows a terrified man clinging to the sides of a steep shaft to avoid falling into a pit. Kevorkian comments, "We contemplate and face it [death] with great apprehension, profound fear, and terror. Sparing no financial or physical sacrifice, pleading wantonly and unashamedly, clutching any hope of salvation through medicine or prayer."[1]

It was Kevorkian's method of doing research that first earned him the nickname Dr. Death. While working as a doctor in training, he would photograph the corneas of dying patients. He learned from these photographs that, as someone dies, the blood vessels in the cornea quickly fade from view.

The medical world recognized the usefulness of this information. But Kevorkian's coworkers disliked his method of obtaining the information. He encouraged their disapproval by referring to his search for moribund patients as the "death rounds" and wearing a black armband. However, his behavior may merely have been the bravado of a young man in an unconventional field of study. He was a pathologist, someone who studies the effects of disease on tissues and body fluids. Death is one of the effects of disease. Some argue that it was natural for him to take a clinical interest in its signs.

OBSESSED WITH DEATH?

Kevorkian's preoccupation with death, however, seemed to go beyond the bounds of clinical interest to some. Claiming that he wanted to salvage some good from death, he tried to interest the medical profession in performing medical experiments on condemned prisoners as they were being executed. In a 1958 paper, he proposed that researchers should experiment on the still-living bodies of heavily sedated convicts. When finished, they could dispatch them by means of a lethal injection. Such a procedure, he said, would greatly lower the costs of research and increase the chances of finding new cures.

Kevorkian's proposed project received no significant support and considerable negative publicity. The chairman of the pathology department in which he worked asked him to either stop publicizing these ideas or give up his job. Kevorkian quit and found another position. Soon, Kevorkian had to accept that the authorities would never let him experiment on dying convicts.

Kevorkian now turned his attention to transfusing blood from people who had just died into living people in need of blood. He was unable to interest his new colleagues in this idea, however.

Hero or Villain?

Wesley J. Smith thinks that Kevorkian is arrogant, self-serving, and murderous. He states, "It is important to reiterate here that, contrary to the usual media descriptions, most of Kevorkian's victims were not terminally ill. Of the known 130 or so suicides that Kevorkian facilitated, about 70 percent of the people involved were disabled and depressed, the majority of them women. This is not surprising given Kevorkian's disdain for disabled people. He once called quadriplegics and paraplegics who were not suicidal 'pathological.'"[2]

In the late 1970s, Kevorkian proposed taking healthy organs from executed criminals to give to people who needed them. Legislators in Kansas, Oklahoma, Texas, and California briefly considered the idea. Their interest did not last, however. They soon joined with other states in rejecting Kevorkian's proposals.

In his professional writings, Kevorkian pointed out that the attempt to stave off death can be worse than death itself. As a doctor, he had firsthand knowledge of how modern medical advances could prolong life beyond the point at which it is meaningful and even endurable. In *Prescription: Medicide*, a book he wrote in 1991, he described a woman in an advanced stage of cancer:

> *The poor wretch stared up at me with yellow eyeballs sunken in their atrophic [sunken] sockets. Her yellow teeth were ringed by chapping and parched lips to form an involuntary, almost sardonic "smile" of death. It seemed as though she was pleading for help and death at the same time. Out of sheer empathy alone I could have helped her die with satisfaction. From that moment on, I was sure that doctor–assisted euthanasia and suicide are and always were ethical, no matter what anyone says or thinks.* [3]

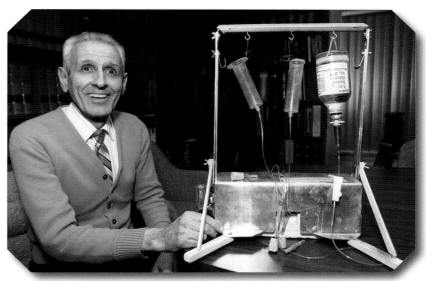

Dr. Jack Kevorkian posing with his "suicide machine,"
which he used to help patients end their lives.

PLANNED DEATH CLINICS

Did Kevorkian's desire to relieve the suffering
of this woman and others like her motivate him to
help people escape misery? Or did an obsession
with death lead him to prey on depressed people?
Kevorkian claims that he had the highest motives
for helping people die. In 1988, he wrote "The Last
Fearsome Taboo: Medical Aspects of Planned Death"
for *Medicine and Law*. In this article, he proposed
opening Planned Death clinics, where terminally

ill patients could choose peaceful and dignified deaths. He proposed that these patients could also choose to aid humanity by submitting themselves to experimentation under irreversible general anesthesia. He felt that experimenting on living humans would save money while speeding up medical advances. These benefits would give meaning to people's deaths.

Kevorkian's new proposal met with the same failure as his previous ideas. Therefore, he carried on his mission without official permission. He tried to advertise for clients in a local medical bulletin. The bulletin rejected the ad. Nonetheless,

Dr. Kevorkian's Suicide Machine

To avoid being accused of murder, Dr. Kevorkian made it possible for his clients to cause their own deaths. He devised a method that consisted of three bottles hanging from a metal frame. Each bottle had a syringe that was connected to an intravenous line in a person's arm. The first bottle held saline solution. This harmless solution kept the vein open to receive the other drugs. The second bottle contained barbiturates that induced sleep. The third was filled with a mixture of potassium chloride (a substance that instantly stops the heart) and a muscle relaxant (a medication that prevents painful spasms).

Kevorkian started the drip of saline solution into the client's vein. The client then activated a switch that released the barbiturates into his or her body. This voluntary act showed that the client accepted responsibility for the procedure. When this medication took effect, the person's falling arm triggered the flow of the potassium chloride. This last step was designed to ensure that the person had fallen asleep before the potassium chloride stopped the heart. The person generally died two to six minutes later.

stories about Kevorkian began to appear in the newspapers, and people began to seek him out. He "treated" his first "patient," Janet Adkins, in 1990. Adkins was a 54-year-old woman diagnosed with Alzheimer's disease.

KEVORKIAN AND THE LAW

Law officials tried repeatedly to end Kevorkian's career. At the time, Michigan (where Kevorkian practiced euthanasia) had no law against assisting suicides. However, he was charged with murder or manslaughter a number of times. All through these trials, right-to-die groups supported Kevorkian. Members of the Hemlock Society testified on his behalf and staged demonstrations for him. Many relatives of the people who committed suicide were also on his side. Sometimes, however, the backing of friends and relatives produced more problems. They were accused of

Kevorkian Talks About His Work

Remembering his feelings after he assisted Janet Adkins to commit suicide, Kevorkian said, "I was so jangled emotionally. You panic because you—is it going well? ... You know, when you're doing something for the first time and nobody else in the country is doing it, you get scared."

He also told a reporter, "She [Janet Adkins] was very calm. She dreaded what would have come. I would too. I don't want to die of Alzheimer's—smeared with your own urine and feces, don't know who you are. Come on!"[4]

joining with Kevorkian in pressuring their friends and relatives to die.

Unable to imprison Kevorkian, law officials and medical boards tried various ways to prevent him from helping people commit suicide. The state board of medicine revoked his Michigan medical license. This meant that he could no longer obtain drugs that would end his patients' lives. Instead, he began to use carbon monoxide. In 1993, when he helped three people kill themselves in one week, the Michigan legislature rushed through a law against assisted suicide. When he was tried under this new law, the jury acquitted him.

Right-to-life groups opposed Kevorkian. Many, but not all, of these opponents were members of fundamentalist religious groups. Not Dead Yet, a group of activists for disabled people, worked against Kevorkian's campaign for assisted suicide. They felt that approval of assisted suicide made disabled people feel that they should kill themselves to avoid being burdens.

KEVORKIAN DEFEATS HIMSELF

Thomas Youk was suffering from Lou Gehrig's disease. This disease drastically weakens muscles and eventually ends in total paralysis and death. Youk was too incapacitated to inject himself with a lethal substance. In 1998, Kevorkian did it for him. The court considered this murder.

Kevorkian could not escape this charge. He had videotaped Youk's death and allowed the producers of the TV show *60 Minutes* to air the tape. Viewers saw Kevorkian injecting the substance that killed Thomas Youk. Judge Jessica Cooper told him, "You had the audacity to go on national television, show the world what you did and dare the legal system to stop you. Well, sir, consider yourself stopped."[5] Kevorkian was sentenced to prison for 10 to 25 years.

Is the Jury Still Out?

The controversy over Kevorkian's actions continues. Right-to-die advocates campaigned for his release. Although Kevorkian was released from prison in June 2007, his release was due to health problems he was experiencing, not the efforts of his allies in the assisted-suicide debate.

Dr. Kevorkian's Release

In the summer of 2007, Dr. Kevorkian was released from prison. Although advocates of doctor-assisted suicide had been pushing for his release for years, he was ultimately let out of jail for health reasons. Kevorkian suffers from a variety of ailments, including diabetes, hepatitis C, and high blood pressure. He has told reporters that he will probably not try to end his life by doctor-assisted suicide.[6]

Kevorkian's opponents still have a very negative opinion of him. Wesley J. Smith is a senior fellow at the Discovery Institute and an attorney for the International Task Force on Euthanasia and Assisted Suicide. He has continued to accumulate evidence against Kevorkian and has pointed out that most of Kevorkian's "victims" were not terminally ill. He contends that five of the people were not even sick. Wesley also pointed to the fact that Kevorkian actually removed the kidneys of Joseph Tushkowski, a quadriplegic man whom he had helped commit suicide. Kevorkian then called a press conference and offered the organs to anyone who needed them. Wesley considered this act a form of bizarre self-promotion and a slap in the public's face. Kevorkian's supporters insist that he wanted some benefit to come from Tushkowski's death. Perhaps there will never be a public consensus on Kevorkian's character and actions. Reviewing his history and reflecting on his personality should, however, help individuals decide how they feel about assisted suicide. ⁓

Dr. Kevorkian was released from prison in 2007.

Terri Schiavo before she suffered catastrophic brain damage

TERRI SCHIAVO

*P*assive voluntary euthanasia is legal
throughout the United States. The
majority of U.S. citizens state that, in certain
circumstances, patients or their designated
representatives should be able to refuse treatment

that might prolong their lives without restoring normal functioning. Many religious opponents of other forms of euthanasia say that it is all right to stop treatment on someone who is either brain-dead or in a vegetative state. Although Terri Schiavo's case seemed to fit the conditions in which passive euthanasia was permissible, the attempt to carry it out was met with a storm of protest.

The Collapse

Early in the morning of February 25, 1990, 26-year-old Terri Schiavo fell in the hallway of her home in St. Petersburg, Florida. Her heart stopped beating for several minutes, interrupting the oxygen flow to her brain. Initially, Terri was in a coma. When she came out of the coma, she could breathe, grimace, and make sounds—but apparently could not think. Most of the neurologists who saw Terri considered the few responses she made to her surroundings to be only reflexes and concluded that she was in a persistent vegetative state. None of the doctors knew what caused Terri's heart to stop beating.

A court appointed Terri's husband, Michael Schiavo, as her surrogate decision maker, the person who would make the important decisions that she was incapable of making for herself. During the first few years after her collapse, Michael approved a variety of treatments and rehabilitation programs to restore Terri's functioning. Her condition, however, did not improve.

FAMILY CONFLICT

In 1993, Terri's parents, the Schindlers, began to ask for more control over Terri's treatment. They sued to have Michael removed from his position as their daughter's surrogate decision maker. A law official reviewed Terri's case and reported that he found no evidence that Michael was not a caring guardian.

In 1994, Michael accepted the medical opinion that Terri was in a persistent vegetative state. After consulting with her doctor, he agreed that any treatment to cure or improve her condition should be halted. In 1998, he petitioned to have Terri's feeding tube removed.

THE FAMILY RIFT WIDENS

In November 1998, Terri's parents learned that one of the examinations given Terri showed that she

Terri Schiavo, right, gets a kiss from her mother, Mary Schindler, who fought to keep Terri alive.

had sustained bone injuries. They accused Michael of abusing her. A doctor, however, stated that the injuries were probably caused by the fall she took when her heart stopped and by subsequent attempts to revive her.

The guardian *ad litem* (a guardian appointed by the court) reported to the court that Terri was in a

"Highly competent, scientifically based physicians using recognized measures and standards have deduced, within a high degree of medical certainty, that Theresa is in a persistent vegetative state. ... When awake, she sometimes groans, makes noises that emulate laughter or crying, and may appear to track movement. But the scientific medical literature and the reports this GAL [Guardian *Ad Litem*] obtained from highly respected neuro-science researchers indicate that these activities are common and characteristic of persons in a persistent vegetative state."[1]

—*statement by Terri's guardian ad litem, Jay Wolfson*

vegetative state and had no chance of improvement. He also advised the court to deny Michael's request for the removal of Terri's feeding tube. The guardian pointed out that Terri's wishes on this matter were not known and that Michael's request might have been motivated by the desire to inherit his wife's money. Michael testified that Terri had told him and several members of his family that she would rather die than be left in a vegetative state. When other witnesses backed up this statement, the court ruled to grant Michael's petition. In 2001, Terri's feeding tube was removed. Her parents appealed, and two days later, it was reinserted until the case could be heard in court.

THE SCHINDLERS FIGHT BACK

During this trial in 2002, two neurologists selected by Michael, two selected by the Schindlers

(Dr. William Hammesfahr and Dr. William Maxfield), and one selected by the court reviewed Terri's medical condition. The two neurologists chosen by the Schindlers reported that Terri was not in a vegetative state but in a minimally conscious state. They claimed that people in minimally conscious states can improve significantly if given proper therapy. The neurologists chosen by Michael and the court claimed that Terri was in a persistent vegetative state.

To support their claim that Terri was conscious of her surroundings, the Schindlers videotaped Dr. Hammesfahr's examination of her. The examination took approximately four hours, but the Schindlers showed only about four minutes of it. Dr. Hammesfahr reported that Terri smiled at her parents, attempted to speak, and made noises as though trying to sing to music played during

Report by Dr. William Hammesfahr

After examining Terri, Dr. Hammesfahr made the following observations:

"The first part of this exam included observing her interactions with her mother and her father. Here she was clearly aware of them and attempted to interact with them. ... I asked the mother to bring a tape of piano music. Two separate pieces were listened to. The first she appeared aware of the sound, but would not sing or interact significantly. The second she did interact making sounds with the music. She stopped making these sounds, when the music stopped."[2]

the exam. On the basis of his observations, Dr. Hammesfahr said that Terri could benefit from therapy. The presiding judge, George Greer, felt that the videotape taken of the exam did not support Dr. Hammesfahr's findings. Dr. Hammesfahr's opinions were also contradicted by the many doctors who had treated Terri since 1990. The judge ruled to have her feeding tube removed.

TERRI'S FATE BECOMES A PUBLIC AND POLITICAL ISSUE

The case received a great deal of publicity. Right-to-life groups supported the Schindlers, while death-with-dignity activists supported Michael. Some of these groups gathered outside Terri's hospital to voice their opinions. The members of the right-to-life groups were mainly fundamentalist Christians. Their stand against

"I urge all those who honor Terri Schiavo to work together to build a culture of life where all Americans are welcomed, valued and protected, especially those who live at the mercy of others. The essence of civilization is that the strong have a duty to protect the weak. In cases where there are serious doubts and questions, the presumption should be in the favor of life."[3]

—*President George W. Bush*

allowing Terri to die was based on the belief that only God has the right to take human life.

Many right-to-life groups supported President George W. Bush and looked to him to defend their values. The governor of Florida at the time was the president's brother, Jeb Bush. Like his brother, Governor Bush also relied on the votes of the members of right-to-life groups. When Terri's feeding tube was again removed in October 2003, he directed that it be reinserted. The Florida Supreme Court declared this directive to be unconstitutional. The U.S. Supreme Court backed the Florida Supreme

Memories of Terri

After Terri's death, CNN showed a videotape in which her friends and relatives shared memories of what she was like before her collapse. Paula Zahn, CNN anchor, organized their remarks and provided background information about Terri and her friends.

Zahn introduced the program: "She was born on December 3, 1963, Theresa Marie, named after Saint Teresa of Avila, older sister of Bobby Jr. and Suzanne, the three children of Robert and Mary Schindler, their home, a middle-class Colonial in the suburbs of northwest Philadelphia."

Bobby Schindler, brother of Terri Schiavo: "We had a big family. And all the holidays and Christmas, we'd just spend those times with the family, and they are times that I'll never forget."

Zahn: "Terri shared everything with her friends, her love of romance novels. Danielle Steel was a favorite author, her crushes on David Cassidy and Paul Michael Glaser from 'Starsky & Hutch.' ... She loved the movie 'An Officer and a Gentleman.' Terri and her friends would watch it over and over again. But it was Terri's love for animals that everyone remembers."[4]

Court's decision. A new order was issued for the tube to be removed on March 18, 2005.

When that day arrived and the tube was removed, President Bush tried to act on behalf of the Schindlers. Both houses of Congress passed a bill that allowed a U.S. District Court to review the case, and President Bush signed it. The court denied the request to have the feeding tube reinserted. The Schindlers then appealed to another district court. That court, too, refused their appeal. The Schindlers also petitioned the U.S. Supreme Court, which refused to intervene. After a few more legal efforts, the Schindlers gave up. Terri died of dehydration on March 31, 2005.

THE POLITICAL IMPLICATIONS

Many people who followed the case were appalled to see the federal government interfere in a private family concern. Democrats felt that the Bush administration became involved in order to please his supporters. They pointed out that many of these supporters believed their church's tenets regarding abortion and euthanasia should be the law of the land. When Bush conceded to them, critics claimed that he was not keeping a proper separation between church and state and was thus violating an important principle of the U.S. Constitution. Some Republicans objected that the government's intervention contradicted the Republican principle that the government should not control private matters.

The Reactions of a Disability Group Leader

Some leaders of disability groups feel that the courts were intrusive in allowing Terri to die. They see it as an example of leaders imposing the solution of death on the issue of dealing with disabled people. Mary Johnson, founder and editor of *Ragged Edge* magazine, points out that there was a difference of medical opinion regarding Terri's awareness of herself and her surroundings. She feels that Terri should have had more protection and proposes "a moratorium on the removal of food

The Results of the Autopsy

On June 15, 2005, Dr. Jon Thogmartin released the results of Terri's autopsy. He reported that her condition was consistent with that of someone who was in a persistent vegetative state. Her brain was about half the size of a normal brain. He stated, "No amount of therapy or treatment would have regenerated [replaced] the massive loss of neurons [nerve cells]."[5]

and water from people diagnosed in a 'persistent vegetable state' or 'minimally conscious state'"[6] until their conditions can be established by new and better diagnostic techniques.

The Results of the Controversy

Has society learned anything from the case of Terri Schiavo? What processes, if any, should be put in place to avoid a similar situation and controversy in the future? Terri's death might have meaning if it leads people to carefully examine their society's attitude about diagnosis and treatment of brain-damaged individuals. ⌐

Many protestors gathered outside Terri's hospital to voice their opinions.

People line up outside the U.S. Supreme Court
to hear a case on assisted suicide.

ASSISTED SUICIDE AND
A DEMOCRATIC SOCIETY

*I*n April 2005, shortly after Terri Schiavo died, a Harris poll was conducted to study current attitudes toward euthanasia and assisted suicide. Pollsters interviewed 1,010 U.S. adults by telephone. The results of this poll showed that more than two-thirds of these adults think that physician-assisted suicide should be legal. Seventy-two percent of the respondents said their wills require the medical staff to remove life-support systems such as feeding tubes if they are irreversibly unconscious. Compared with polls on the same subjects taken in previous years, approval of active as well as passive euthanasia seemed to be increasing among U.S. citizens.

SOCIAL ASPECTS OF ASSISTED SUICIDE

Many supporters of assisted suicide point to things such as the Harris poll as evidence that assisted suicide should be legal in the United States. They argue that a law in favor of doctor-assisted suicide would affect only those who want the procedure. It would not force anyone to choose death. On the other hand, they say that a law against doctor-assisted suicide would violate the rights of those who, under certain circumstances, might want such a choice to be available.

Regardless of their political affiliation, a number of people point out that it is naive to assume that a law allowing doctor-assisted suicide would necessarily involve only the subject's choice. They add that even the legal status of passive euthanasia can be discriminatory. Leaders of groups that work for the rights of disabled people are especially concerned about the effects that the Patient Determination Act has had on members of their community.

FURTHER QUESTIONS ABOUT THE TERRI SCHIAVO CASE

Critics express reservations about passive euthanasia as well. They point out that its legalization allows society to eliminate hospital patients who cannot communicate. Some people questioned whether Terri's earlier statement that she would rather die than be kept on life-support equipment reflected her desires once she was in that situation. In her essay, "After Terri Schiavo," Mary Johnson quotes David Jayne, a Lou Gehrig's disease patient:

> If someone had told me prior to the diagnosis that I would be totally paralyzed, fed by a feeding tube, communicate via computer with a voice synthesizer and tethered to a ventilator,

[yet] that I would find more meaning in life and living, I am certain [I would have thought] that person telling me such a tale was insane.[2]

Nonetheless, he chose to live under such conditions and claims that he does not regret having done so.

Joan Didion, a well-known journalist, essayist, and novelist, shares Johnson's views. She feels that everyone should be protected against an unquestioning acceptance of some of the principles of right-to-die activists. She was dissatisfied with the general assumption that Terri, while still mentally competent, had expressed a clear and considered desire for death should she ever be helpless and apparently unresponsive. Everyone, Didion says, has at times expressed a desire to die rather than be kept artificially alive by a machine.

To write this momentary wish down as an official "living will" could easily be a tragic mistake. Didion cites studies by Angela Fagerlin, a medical researcher, and Carl E. Schneider, a law professor at the University

"Right now, well over a tenth of all Medicare dollars pay for care provided in the last 30 days of patients' lives. Some of that care is necessary and proper, but much is not. In one survey of 1,400 doctors and nurses, 65 percent admitted providing unnecessary treatment to terminally ill patients. If more Medicare patients used living wills to block such unnecessary and unwanted last-minute procedures, the savings could be substantial."[3]
—*Eric Lindblom, November 1995 Washington Monthly*

A Narrow Escape

Robert Wageman had a hip injury caused by a difficult delivery. When he was five years old, he was examined by Nazi doctors. In a 1994 interview, he tells how his mother overheard the doctors planning to put him to sleep. "[D]uring lunch time, while the, uh, doctors were gone, she, uh, grabbed hold of me, we went down to the Neckar River into the high reeds and there she put my clothes on, and from there on we really went into hiding ..."[5]

of Michigan. These researchers found that "almost a third of such decisions, after periods as short as two years, no longer reflect the wishes of those who made them."[4]

Does Assisted Suicide Threaten the Democratic Way of Life?

Many critics of euthanasia agree that there is a danger in legalizing doctor-assisted suicide and passive euthanasia. They point out that health care in the United States is expensive. For people who have trouble paying for health care, assisted suicide might be the only practical way to avoid a painful and undignified death. Many of these people believe that society regards them as a drain on public resources. This attitude can make them feel that it is their duty to die. Such indirect pressure, critics say, may be the first step toward a society that imposes euthanasia on unwilling subjects.

Not too long ago, such a society existed. During the 1930s and 1940s, Nazi Germany practiced active, involuntary euthanasia on the disabled and other groups that they thought might contaminate the German gene pool. Many opponents of euthanasia fear that legalizing assisted suicide might eventually lead to similar abuse in the United States.

Adherents of euthanasia point out that in spite of the propaganda campaign, the German population resisted this program. The Nazis then carried it out in secret. Supporters of euthanasia argue that legalizing euthanasia is the best way to prevent its abuse. It can then be regulated by guidelines and monitored by medical review boards.

SOME QUESTIONS POSED BY THE DEBATE OVER ASSISTED SUICIDE

The issue of assisted suicide has

Assisted Suicide in the Movies

Many activists for the disabled objected strongly to the 2004 movie *Million Dollar Baby*. In this movie, a talented female boxer opted for assisted suicide when she was paralyzed by an injury to her spinal cord. Activist Marcie Roth, executive director of the National Spinal Cord Injury Association, states that this movie "sends a message that having a spinal cord injury is a fate worse than death."[6] Roth received many letters from the people that she represents complaining of this movie's negative message.

Other activists were even more outspoken. "This movie is a corny, melodramatic assault on people with disabilities,"[7] wrote Stephen Drake on the Web site of a Chicago-based activist group called Not Dead Yet. "It plays out killing as a romantic fantasy and gives emotional life to the 'better dead than disabled' mindset lurking in the heart of the typical (read: nondisabled) audience member."[6]

given rise to a number of questions, including:

❖ Does U.S. society indirectly pressure vulnerable people to choose euthanasia?

❖ Does legalizing doctor-assisted suicide debase the physician and his or her vocation?

❖ Is it cruel to force a person to endure a life that is limited to only basic functions and considered by some to be meaningless and painful?

❖ Is making assisted suicide illegal a violation of a person's autonomy?

These are difficult questions, and the opponents in this debate may never agree with each other. However, regardless of their position on assisted suicide, most people agree that the U.S. health care system should be accessible to everyone and end-of-life care should be improved for all members of society.

Approval for Oregon's Death with Dignity Law

"The Death With Dignity law is part of a broader—and welcome—reinterpretation of the role of medicine. ... The Oregon law deserves to be upheld. It forces us to examine the question of what is special about human life. The answer, I think, is the autonomy and dignity inherent in our individuality—in making hard decisions for ourselves and determining our own destinies. Oregon honors that vision of what is sacred about life."[7]

—*Nicholas Kristof in his July 14, 2004,* New York Times *column "Choosing Death"*

*Author Joan Didion expressed reservations about
passive euthanasia and living wills.*

TIMELINE

1906	1938	1973
The first euthanasia bill is drafted in Ohio. It does not succeed.	The Euthanasia Society of America is founded.	The American Hospital Association approves the Patient Bill of Rights.

1980	1986	1988
The Hemlock Society, which works for legal change and publicizes information about obtaining a painless death, is founded.	On April 24, an appeals court grants Elizabeth Bouvia, a quadriplegic, the right to die. Bouvia does not exercise this right.	The Unitarian Universalist Association of Congregations passes a resolution in favor of assisted suicide for the terminally ill on June 17.

1974

The Euthanasia Society of America changes its name to the Society for the Right to Die.

1976

On March 31, the New Jersey Supreme Court rules Karen Ann Quinlan's respirator could be removed.

1976

In May, California passes the first Natural Death Act, legalizing living wills.

1990

The American Medical Association decides that a doctor can take moribund and comatose patients off life support.

1990

On June 4, Dr. Jack Kevorkian helps Janet Adkins, a woman with Alzheimer's disease, to commit suicide.

1990

On June 25, the Supreme Court rules that competent adults have the constitutional right to refuse medical treatment.

TIMELINE

1991

According to a nationwide Gallup poll, 75 percent of Americans approve of living wills.

1993

Right-to-die activists found Compassion in Dying, which counsels the terminally ill, in the state of Washington.

1994

On November 8, Oregon residents vote in favor of the Death with Dignity Act.

1999

On April 13, a Michigan judge sentences Kevorkian to 10 to 25 years in prison for second-degree murder of Youk.

2001

On April 10, the Netherlands legalizes voluntary euthanasia.

2001

On November 5, Attorney General Ashcroft blocks Oregon's Death with Dignity Act. He rules that it violates federal drug laws.

1994	1998	1998
Advance directives becomes legal in all U.S. states and the District of Columbia.	On March 24, the first publicly recognized physician-assisted suicide occurs in Oregon.	On November 22, CBS program *60 Minutes* shows a video clip of Jack Kevorkian giving Thomas Youk a lethal injection.

2002	2005	2007
On April 17, U.S. District Judge Jones decides that the U.S. Justice Department cannot overturn Oregon's Death with Dignity Act.	On March 18, Judge Greer orders Terri Schiavo's feeding tube to be disconnected for the third and final time.	On June 1, Dr. Kevorkian is released from prison.

ESSENTIAL FACTS

AT ISSUE

Opposed

❖ Life is sacred. Only God can destroy life.

❖ Medical diagnoses are sometimes mistaken. Legalization of euthanasia might lead to unnecessary deaths.

❖ Euthanasia may be abused. Members of vulnerable groups, such as the elderly or the disabled, may be pressured into requesting euthanasia.

❖ Euthanasia would damage the doctor's professional integrity, changing the doctor from a healer to an executioner.

In Favor

❖ Humans have the right to autonomy. Competent people should be allowed to choose how they will die.

❖ Common humanity requires a doctor to help a person die when that person's life becomes too painful.

❖ Unauthorized euthanasia already occurs. Legalizing euthanasia will lead to better regulation and reduce abuse of the process.

❖ Terminally ill patients sometimes have a duty to die in order to relieve caretaking relatives of extraordinary burdens.

KEY LEGISLATION

May 1976
California passed the first Natural Death Act. This act legalized living wills and protected the physicians who honored them from lawsuits.

November 8, 1994
Oregon residents voted in favor of the Death with Dignity Act, becoming the only state to legalize physician-assisted suicide.

April 10, 2001
The Netherlands legalized voluntary euthanasia. It was the first and only country so far to do so.

Quotes

Opposed

"The medical profession has always sternly set its face against a measure that would inevitably pave the way to the grossest abuse and would degrade them to the position of executioners."—*The British Medical Journal*

"It is within God's purview [scope or range] alone to decide on the moment when the individual is to share that life which lies beyond death in a world restored to a splendor even greater than its pristine [unspoiled] purity. Within the context of this certain hope, mercy killing runs squarely against the grain of the will of a gracious Creator."—*"Report on Euthanasia with Guiding Principles," prepared by a Lutheran Commission on Theology and Church Relations*

In Favor

"[I]n all cases of hopeless and painful illness, it should be the recognized duty of the medical attendant, whenever so desired by the patient, to administer chloroform or such other anesthetic as may by-and-by supersede chloroform—so as to destroy consciousness at once, and put the sufferer to a quick and painless death."
—*Samuel D. Williams*

"That our current American model of medical care, which is dominated [controlled] by business and profit and managed care, might see good palliative care as particularly expensive and physician-assisted suicide as relatively cheap is, I think, a reason not to make physician-assisted suicide illegal but to reform our system of financing health care."—*Lawrence Hartmann. M.D.*

ADDITIONAL RESOURCES

SELECT BIBLIOGRAPHY

Betzold, Michael. *Appointment with Doctor Death*. Troy, Michigan: Momentum Books, Ltd., 1995.

Caplan, Arthur L., James J. McCartney, and Dominic A. Sisti, eds. *The Case of Terri Schiavo*. Amherst, New York: Prometheus Books, 2006.

Foley, Kathleen, M.D., and Herbert Hendin, M.D., eds. *The Case against Assisted Suicide: For the Right to End-of-Life Care*. Baltimore and London: The John Hopkins University Press, 2002.

Hardwig, John. *Is There a Duty to Die? And Other Essays in Medical Ethics*. New York and London: Routledge, 2000.

Larue, Gerald A., Th.D. *Playing God: Fifty Religions' Views on Your Right to Die*. Wakefield, Rhode Island, and London: Moyer Bell, 1996.

Logue, Barbara J. *Last Rights: Death Control and the Elderly in America*. New York: Lexington Books, An Imprint of Macmillan, Inc., 1993.

Moreland, J.P., and Norman L. Geisler. *The Life and Death Debate: Moral Issues of Our Time*. New York: Greenwood Press, 1990.

Woodman, Sue. *Last Rights: The Struggle over the Right to Die*. New York and London: Plenum Press, 1998.

FURTHER READING

Heintze, Carl. *Medical Ethics*. New York: Franklin Watts, 1987.

Landau, Elaine. *Death: Everyone's Heritage*. New York: Julian Messner, 1976.

Yount, Lisa. *Physician-Assisted Suicide and Euthanasia*. New York: Facts on File, 2000.

Web Links

To learn more about assisted suicide, visit ABDO Publishing Company on the World Wide Web at **www.abdopublishing.com**. Web sites about assisted suicide are featured on our Book Links page. These links are routinely monitored and updated to provide the most current information available.

For More Information

For more information on this subject, contact or visit the following organizations.

The Hemlock Society/Compassion and Choices
<http://www.hemlock.org>
PO Box 101810
Denver, CO 80250
The Hemlock Society and Compassion and Choices team up to provide information about end-of-life care and assisted suicide.

Ragged Edge Magazine
<http://www.raggededgemagazine.com>
Ragged Edge is an online magazine focusing on the rights of disabled people, and contains many articles about assisted suicide.

GLOSSARY

academic
Scholarly and intellectual.

administer
To give someone a measured amount of a medication.

advance directive
A legal document signed by a competent person giving instructions about medical and healthcare decisions.

advocate
Somebody who supports something; somebody who acts on behalf of another.

anesthetic
Painkiller.

authorize
To give permission to someone to do something.

autonomy
The capacity to make moral decisions and to act on them.

competent
Able to carry out normal functions effectively.

disabled
Used to describe someone with a condition that makes it difficult to perform some or all the basic tasks of daily life.

dissenter
Someone who disagrees with the beliefs or opinions of a majority.

durable power of attorney
A legal document that allows someone to authorize an agent to make legal decisions for when the person is no longer able to do so themselves.

ethics
The study of moral standards and how they affect conduct.

hospice
A small institution for terminally ill patients where treatment focuses on physical and emotional comfort.

intrinsic
> Belonging to something as one of the basic and essential elements that make it what it is.

libertarian
> Someone who believes that people should have complete freedom of thought and action and should not be subject to the authority of the state.

living will
> A document in which someone declines to be kept alive artificially by life-support systems in case of a terminal illness.

manslaughter
> The unlawful killing of one human being by another without advanced planning.

martyrdom
> When someone dies because of his or her beliefs.

persistent vegetative state
> A chronic state in which someone cannot think, be aware of surroundings, or recognize people.

procedure
> Any means of doing or accomplishing something.

respirator
> A machine used in hospitals to maintain breathing.

traditionalist
> One that follows beliefs and practices established by tradition or custom.

ventilator
> A machine that keeps air moving in and out of the lungs of a patient who cannot breathe normally.

voluntary
> Arising, acting, or resulting from somebody's own choice.

Source Notes

Chapter 1. Choosing How and When to Die
1. Susan Jacoby. "The Right to Die." *AARP Bulletin Online*, Nov. 2005. <http://www.aarp.org/bulletin/yourlife/assisted_suicide.html>.
2. John Jefferson Davis. *Evangelical Ethics: Issues Facing the Church Today*. Phillipsburg, NJ: Presbyterian and Reformed Publishing Company. 170.

Chapter 2. Early Cultures and Euthanasia
1. Ezekiel J. Emanuel. "The History of Euthanasia Debates in the United States and Britain. *Annals of Internal Medicine*. 15 Nov. 1994. <http://www.annals.org/cgi/content/full/121/10/793>
2. *Killing Yourself: the Ethics of Suicide and Euthanasia*. <http://academics. vmi.edu/psy_dr/killing_yourself.htm>.
3. Ezekiel J. Emanuel. "The History of Euthanasia Debates in the United States and Britain. *Annals of Internal Medicine*. 15 Nov. 1994. <http://www.annals.org/cgi/content/full/121/10/793>.
4. Ibid.
5. Kevin Yuill. "The 'right to die'? No, thanks." 19 May 2006. *spiked*, Signet House, London 2000-2007 <http://www.spiked-online.com/index.php?/site/article/207/>.
6. WorldofQuotes.com. <http://www.worldofquotes.com/author/ David-Hume/1/index.html>.
7. "It's Over, Debbie." *A Piece of My Mind*. Ed. Rosanne K. Young. JAMA 1 Jan. 1988. <http://web.missouri.edu/~bondesonw/Debbie. HTM>.
8. Ibid.
9. Ibid.
10. Ibid.

Chapter 3. Religious Arguments against Assisted Suicide
1. Gerald A. Larue, Th.D. *Playing God*. Wakefield, Rhode Island, and London: Moyer Bell, 1996. 98.
2. *Declaration On Euthanasia*, Sacred Congregation for the Doctrine of the Faith. 5 May 1980. <http://catholicinsight.com/online/ political/euthanasia/article_321.shtml>.
3. Gerald A. Larue, Th.D. *Playing God*. Wakefield, Rhode Island & London: Moyer Bell, 1996. 101–102.
4. Ibid. 102.

5. Ibid.
6. Ibid. 138.
7. Ibid. 356.
8. Ibid. 134.
9. Ibid. 356.
10. Ibid. 357.
11. Ibid. 328.
12. Ibid. 367.

Chapter 4. Can a Religious Person Support Assisted Suicide?
1. Arthur J. Droge and James D. Tabor. *A Noble Death: Suicide and Martyrdom among Christians and Jews in Antiquity*. San Francisco: Harper-SanFrancisco, 1992. 1.
2. Ibid. 2.
3. Ibid. 73.
4. Gerald A. Larue, Th.D. *Playing God*. Wakefield, Rhode Island, and London: Moyer Bell, 1996. 182.
5. Ibid. 63.
6. Ibid.
7. Ibid. 9–10.
8. Ibid. 365.

Chapter 5. Ethical Arguments against Assisted Suicide
1. Kevin Yuill. "The 'right to die'? No, thanks." 19 May 2006 *spiked*, Signet House, London 2000-2007. <http://www.spiked-online.com/index.php?/site/article/207/>.
2. Rita L. Marker and Wesley J. Smith. "When Killing Yourself Isn't Suicide" 5 Mar. 2007. National Review Online, 2006-2007. <http://article.nationalreview.com/?q-NGYwNWM4Y-2EwORDji>.
3. "A Debate on Physician-Assisted Suicide." *American Psychiatric Services*. Nov. 1998. <http://psychservices.psychiatryonline.org/cgi/content/full/49/11/1468>.
4. C. Everett Koop. Quoted in *KOOP, The Memoirs of America's Family Doctor*. New York: Random House, 1991. 293.

Source Notes Continued

5. Leon Kass. "'I will Give No Deadly Drug': Why Doctors Must Not Kill." *The Case against Assisted Suicide*. Eds. Kathleen Foley, M.S., and Herbert Hendin, M.D. Baltimore and London: John Hopkins University Press. 2002. 40.

Chapter 6. Ethical Arguments for Assisted Suicide

1. Obituary of James Rachels, Ph.D. *Birmingham News*. 6 Sept. 2003. <http:.www.bradpriddy.com/rachels/obituary.htm>.
2. James Rachels. *Created from Animals*. Oxford: Oxford University Press. <http://www.bradpriddy.com/rachels/cfa.htm>
3. Barbara J. Logue. *Last Rights: Death Control and the Elderly in America*. New York: Maxwell Macmillan International, 1993. 225.
4. John Hardwig, *Is There a Duty to Die? And Other Essays in Medical Ethics*. New York: Routledge. 31.
5. Ibid. 133–134.
6. Ibid. 132.

Chapter 7. Dr. Kevorkian

1. Jack Kevorkian. "A Summary of Dr. Kevorkian's Artwork." <http://www.fansoffieger.com/kevoart.htm>.
2. Wesley J. Smith. "A View to a Kill." nationalreviewON-LINE. 14 Dec. 2005. <http://www.nationalreview.com/smithw/smith200512140825.asp>.
3. Michael Betzold. *Appointment with Doctor Death*. Troy, Michigan: Momentum Books Ltd. 9.
4. Ibid. 48.
5. "'Dr. Death': Pushing the Law." *BBC News*. 28 Nov. 2000. <http://news.bbc.co.uk/2/hi/health/background_briefings/euthanasia/331269.stm>.
6. Kathy Barks Hoffman. "Kevorkian a Free Man after 8 Years in a Michigan Prison." *Associated Press*. 1 June 2007. <http://www.death-withdignity.org/new/new/washingtonpost.12.23.05.asp>.

Chapter 8. Terri Schiavo

1. Jay Wolfson, Dr. P.H., J.D. "Report to Governor Jeb Bush and the 6th Judicial Circuit in the Matter of Theresa Maria Schiavo." WolfsonReport.pdf. 30.
2. William Hammesfahr, Dr. "Complete Report of Dr. William Hammesfahr." 12 Sept. 2002. Liberty to the Captives.

2. William Hammesfahr, Dr. "Complete Report of Dr. William Hammesfahr." 12 Sept. 2002. Liberty to the Captives. <http://libertytothecaptives.net/hammersfahr_dr._report.html>.
3. "Reaction to Schiavo's Death." *Bay News* 9. 31 Mar. 2005. <http://www.baynews9.com/content/36/2005/3/31/7475.html>.
4. Paula Zahn. "The Life of Terri Schiavo." *CNN.com*. 28 Mar. 2005. <http://transcripts.cnn.com/TRANSCRIPTS/0503/28/pzn.01.html>.
5. "Autopsy, No Sign Schiavo Was Abused." *CNN news.com*. 17 June 2005. <http://www.cnn.com/2005/HEALTH/06/15/schiavo.autopsy/>.
6. Mary Johnson. "After Terri Schiavo." *The Case of Terri Schiavo*. Arthur L. Caplan, James J. McCartney, and Dominie Sisto, eds. Amherst, New York: Prometheus Books. 283.

Chapter 9. Assisted Suicide and a Democratic Society
1. Wendy McElroy. "Pro-Lifers Link Euthanasia to Abortion." The Liberator. 10 Nov. 2003. <http://www.liberator.net/articles/McElroyWendy/Pro-Lifers.html>.
2. Mary Johnson. "After Terri Schiavo." *The Case of Terri Schiavo*. Arthur L. Caplan, James J. McCartney, and Dominic A. Sisti, eds. Amherst, New York: Prometheus Books. 280.
3. Eric Lindblom. "Where There's a Living Will . . .". Nov. 1995. <http://findarticles.com/p/article/mi_m1316/is_11_27/ai_54469058>.
4. Joan Didion. "The Case of Theresa Schiavo." *New York Review of Books*, 9 June 2005. <http://www.nybooks.com/articles/18050>.
5. "Robert Wagemann Describes Fleeing from a Clinic where, his Mother Feared, He Was to be Put to Death by Euthanasia." Euthanasia Program. 1994 interview. <http://www.ushmm.org/wlc/article.php?lang=en&ModuleId=10005200>.
6. Sharon Waxman. "'Million Dollar Baby' Plot Twist Draws Controversy." *New York Times*. 3 Feb. 2005. austin360.com. <http://www.austin360.com/movies/content/movies/aasstories/2005_january/3babyprotest.html>.
7. Nicholas Kristoff. "Choosing Death." *New York Times*. 14 July 2004. <http://www.euthanasiaprocon.org/dwdagoodbadlaw.html>.

INDEX

ABOUT THE AUTHOR

Lillian Forman is a former high school teacher of English who now writes and edits educational materials for students. Forman says that what she loves most about her new profession is the opportunity to learn about a wide variety of topics. Forman has also published short stories for children. For her own pleasure, she writes personal essays and poetry.

PHOTO CREDITS

Charles Dharapak/AP Images, cover, 3, 9, 54, 88, 98 (top); Jack Kanthal/AP Images, 6, 97 (top); Serge Ligtenberg/AP Images, 15, 44, 98 (bottom); North Wind Photo Archives, 16, 19, 21, 25, 36; Pier Paolo Cito/AP Images, 26; Issam Diek/AP Images, 31; Barry Thumma/AP Images, 35; Bikas Das/AP Images, 43; Banks/ AP Images, 50; stf/AP Images, 53; Adrian Keating/AP Images, 63, 96; Richard Sheinwald/AP Images, 64, 69, 97 (bottom); Carlos Osorio/AP Images, 75; Schindler Family Photo/AP Images, 76, 79, 99; Chris O'Meara/AP Images, 87; Kathy Willens/AP Images, 95